SUNNY DAYS
IN THE VIRGIN ISLANDS

A TRAVELER'S COLORING BOOK

created & illustrated by Cricky

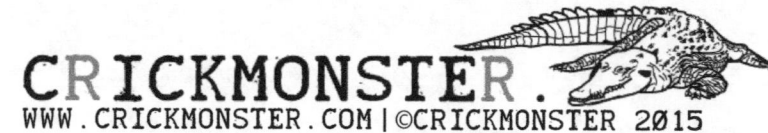

CRICKMONSTER.
WWW.CRICKMONSTER.COM | ©CRICKMONSTER 2015

PAGE GUIDE.

a few things you see on a sunny day in the Virgin Islands...

1. Map of the U.S. and British Virgin Islands

2. Carnival Costume Headdress

3. Spotted Eagle Ray

4. Papaya Tree

5. Green Iguana

6. Bananaquit

7. St. Thomas Tree Boa

8. Rooster

9. Lignum Vitae (Leaves and Flowers)

10. Parrotfish

11. Carnival Costume

12. Caribbean Flamingo

13. Jellyfish

14. Green Sea Turtle with Jellyfish

15. Passionflower

16. Blue Marlin

17. Blue Agave with Prickly Pear Cactuses

18. Common Octopus

19. Fishing Boat on the Beach

20. Flags of the U.S. and British Virgin Islands

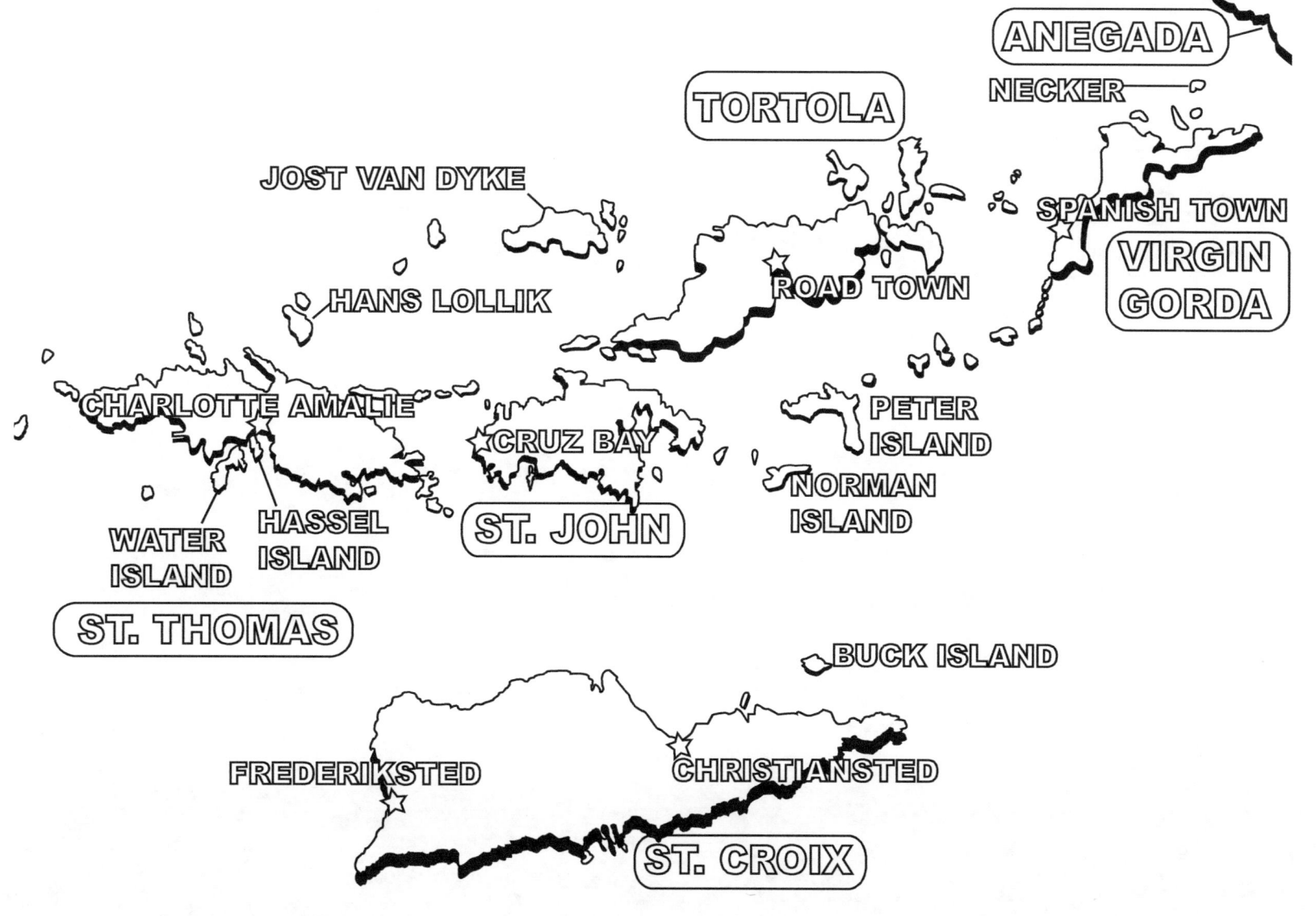

ANEGADA

NECKER

TORTOLA

JOST VAN DYKE

SPANISH TOWN

VIRGIN GORDA

HANS LOLLIK

ROAD TOWN

CHARLOTTE AMALIE

PETER ISLAND

CRUZ BAY

NORMAN ISLAND

ST. JOHN

WATER ISLAND

HASSEL ISLAND

ST. THOMAS

BUCK ISLAND

FREDERIKSTED

CHRISTIANSTED

ST. CROIX

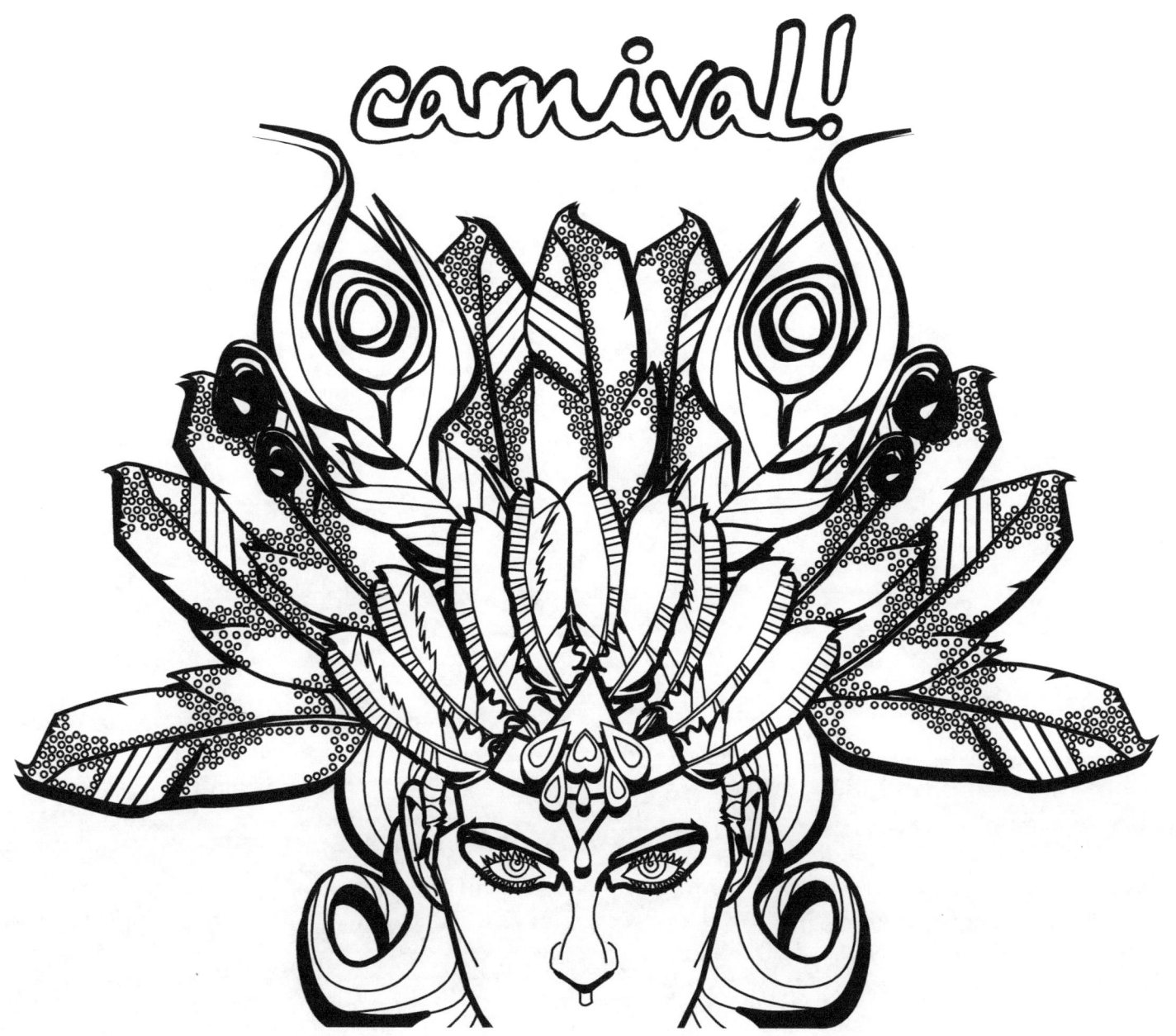

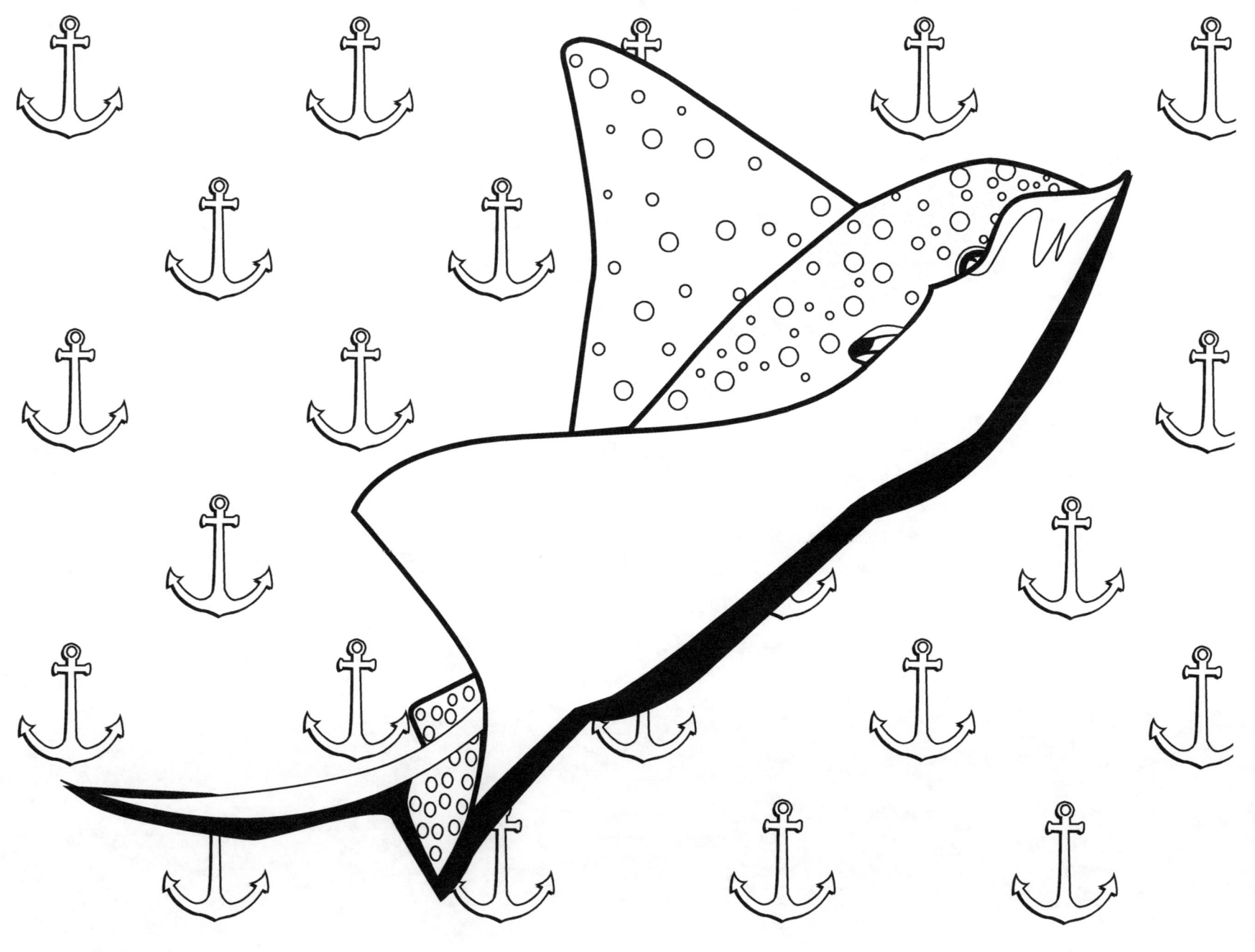

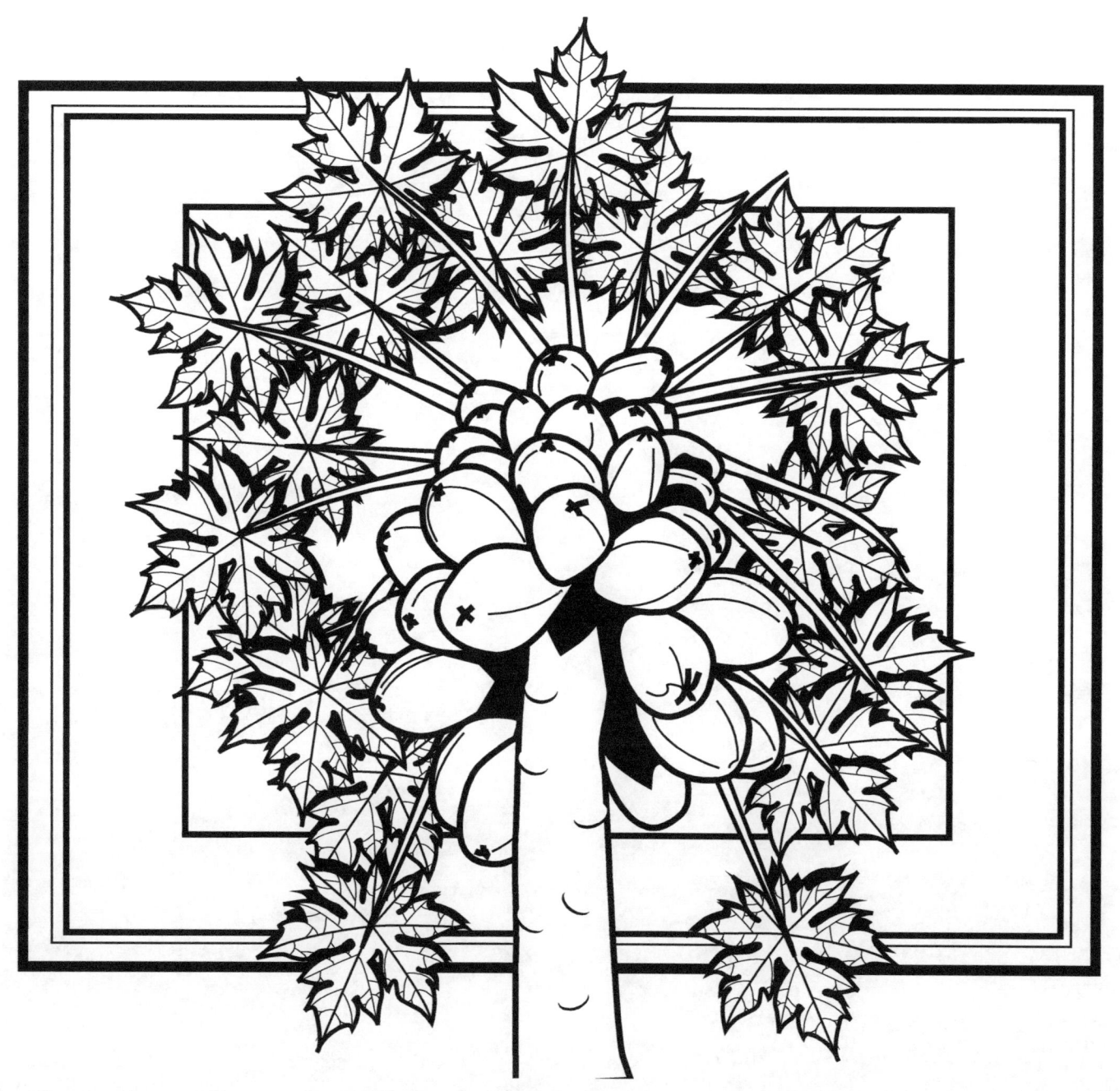

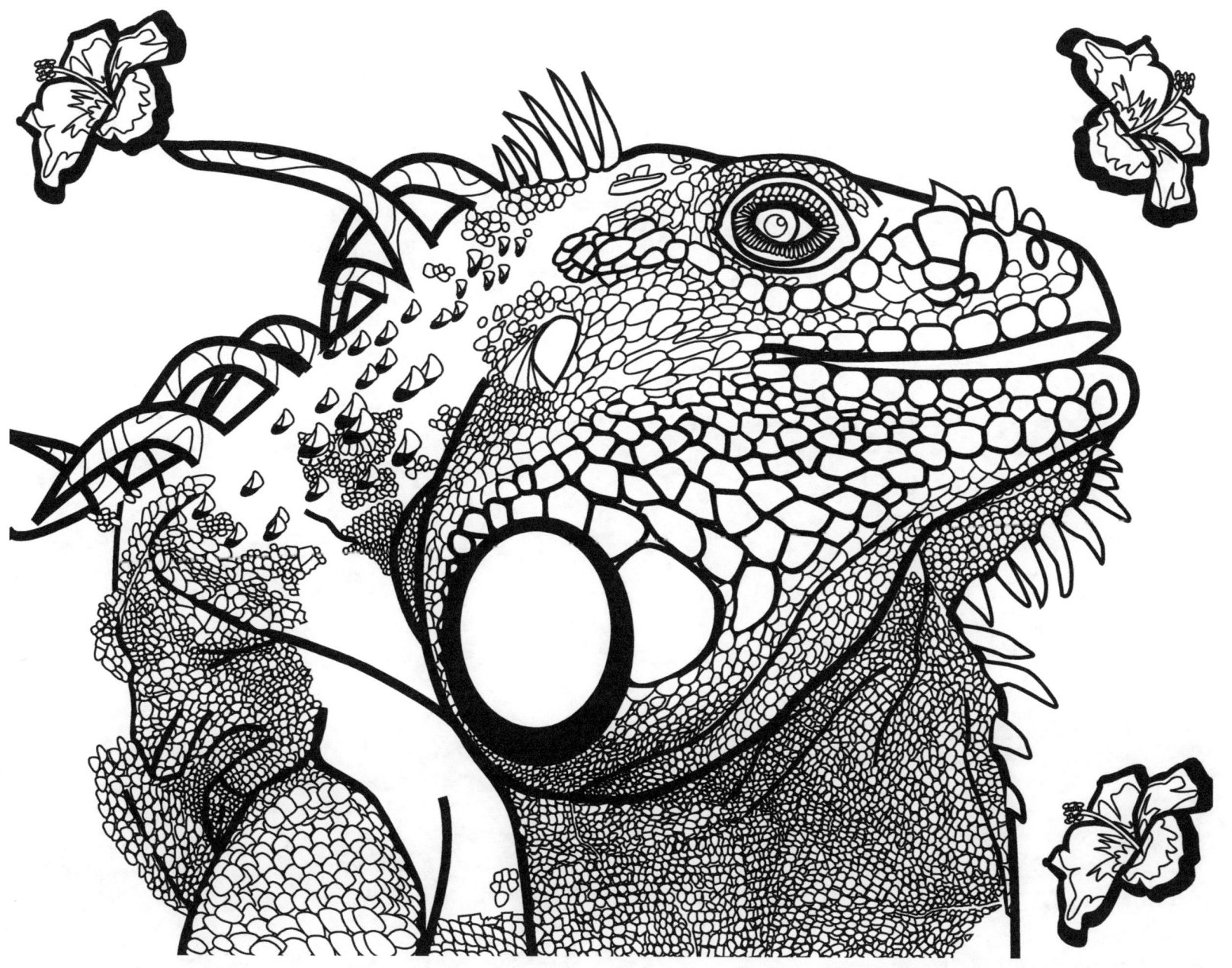

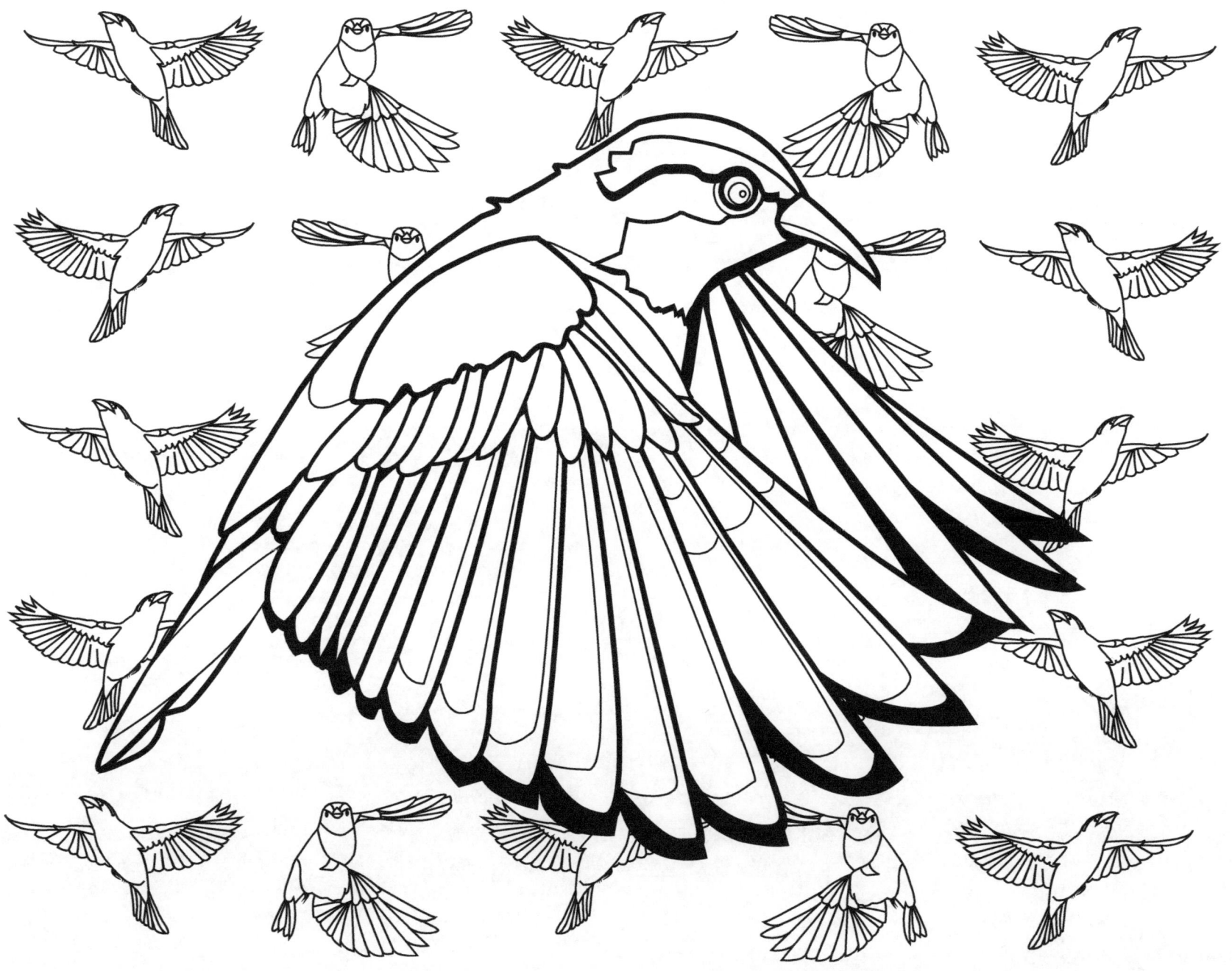

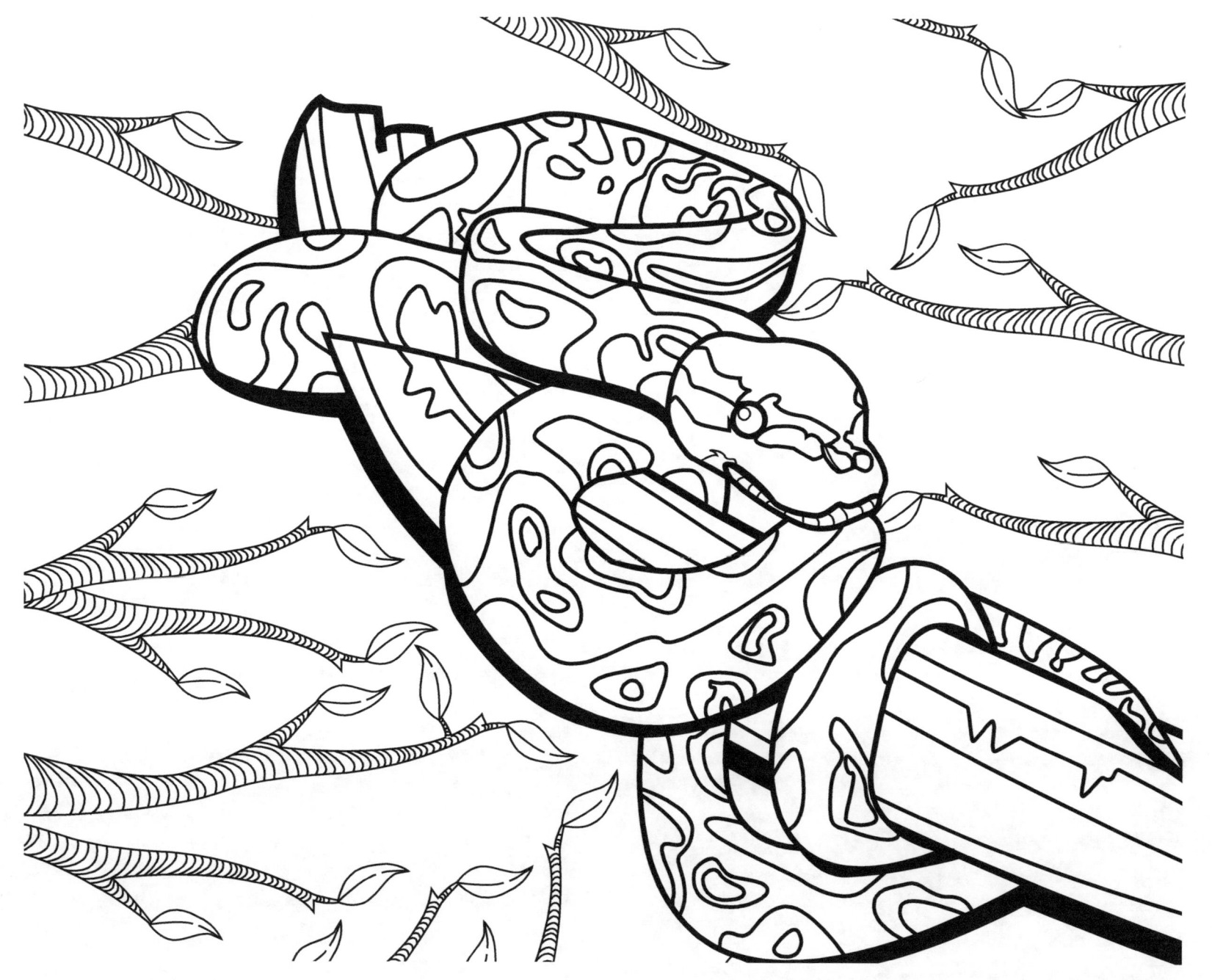

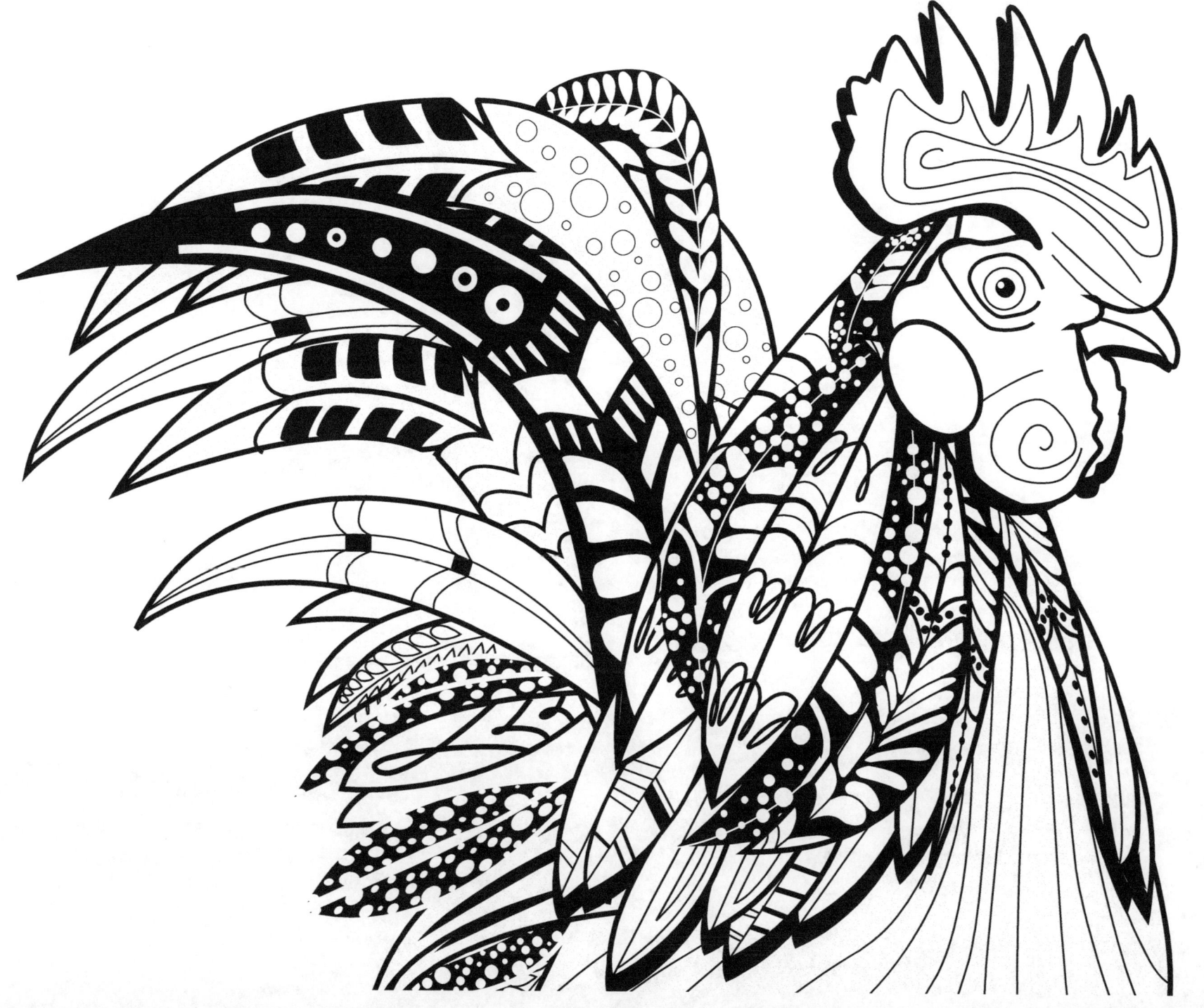

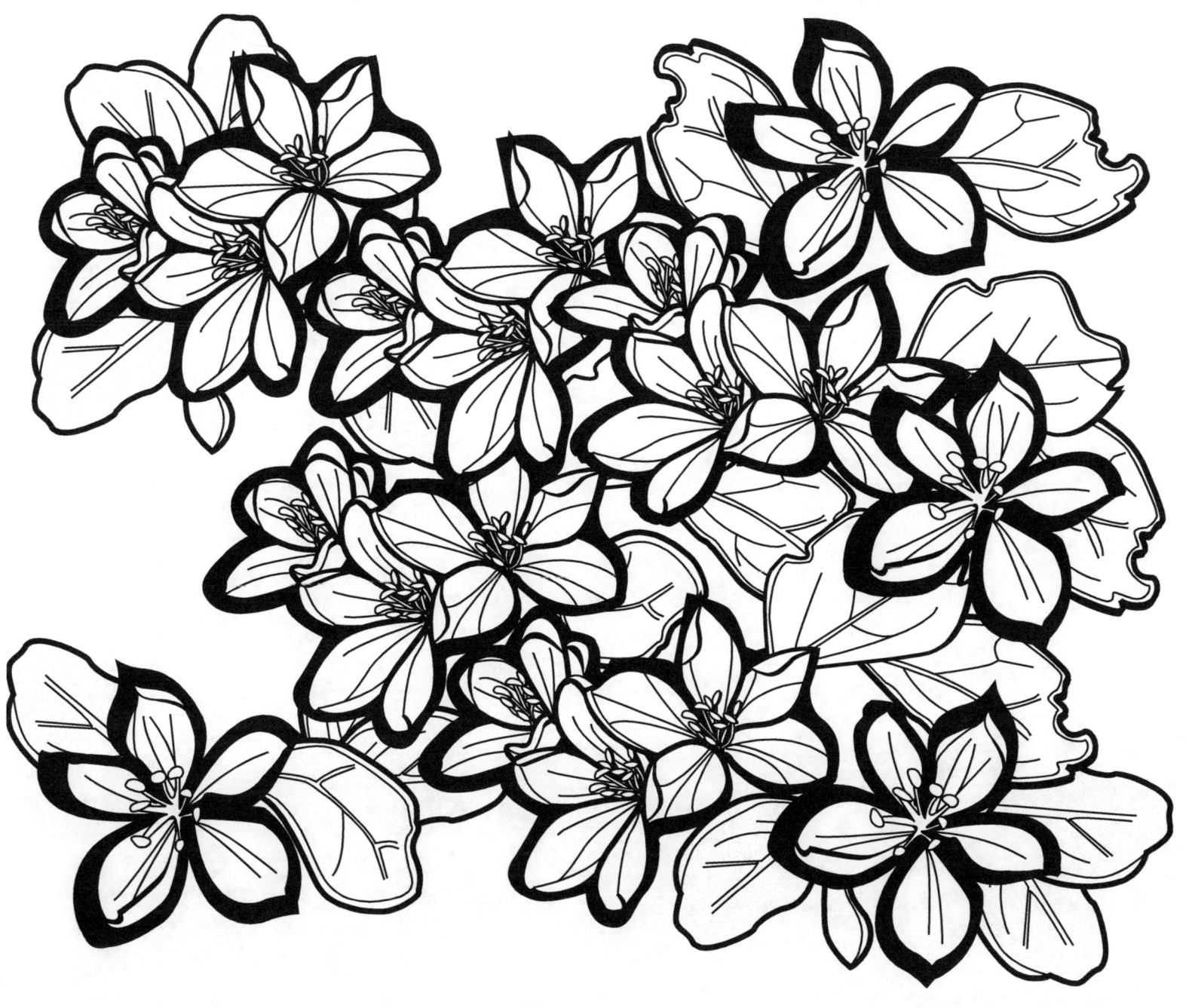

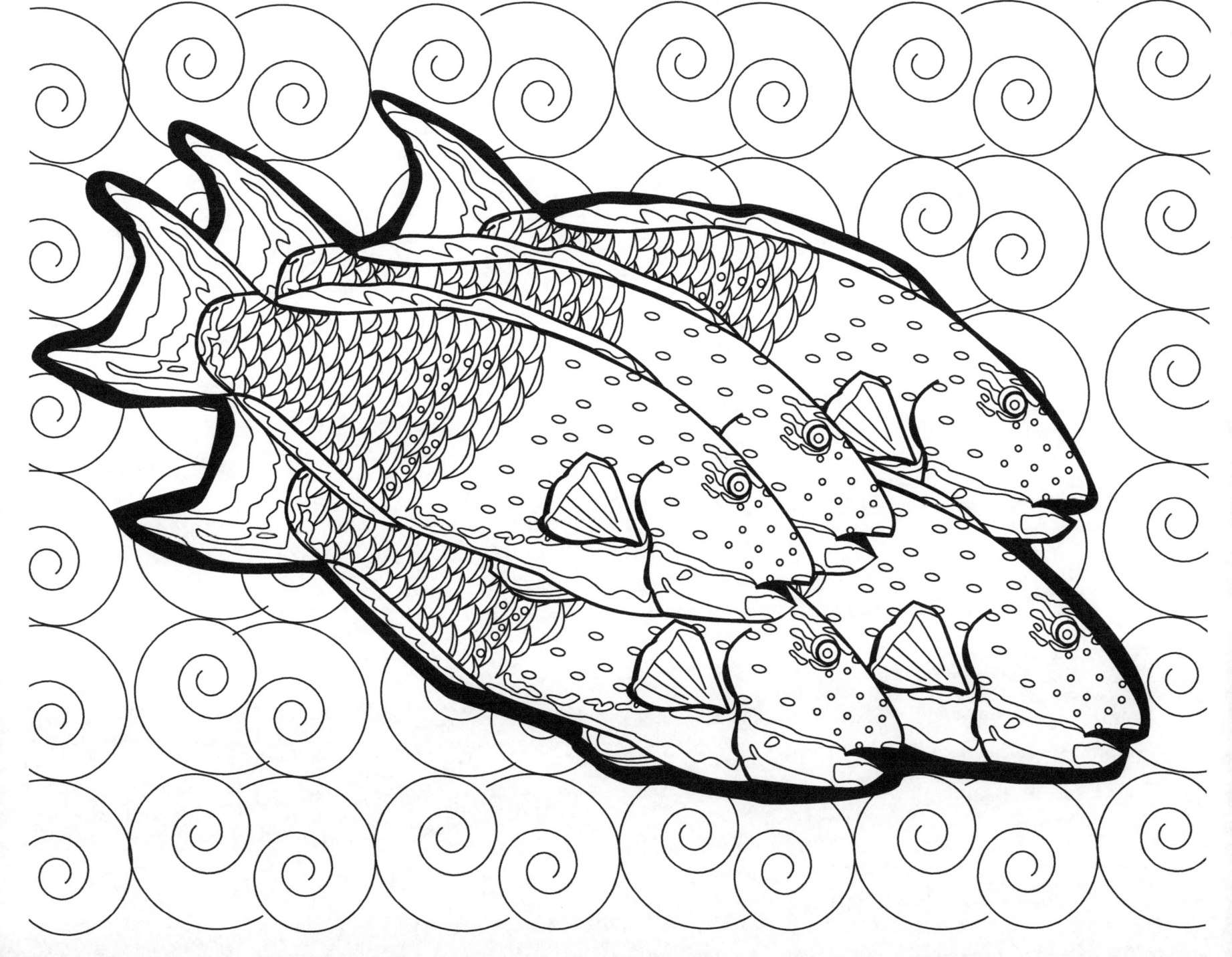

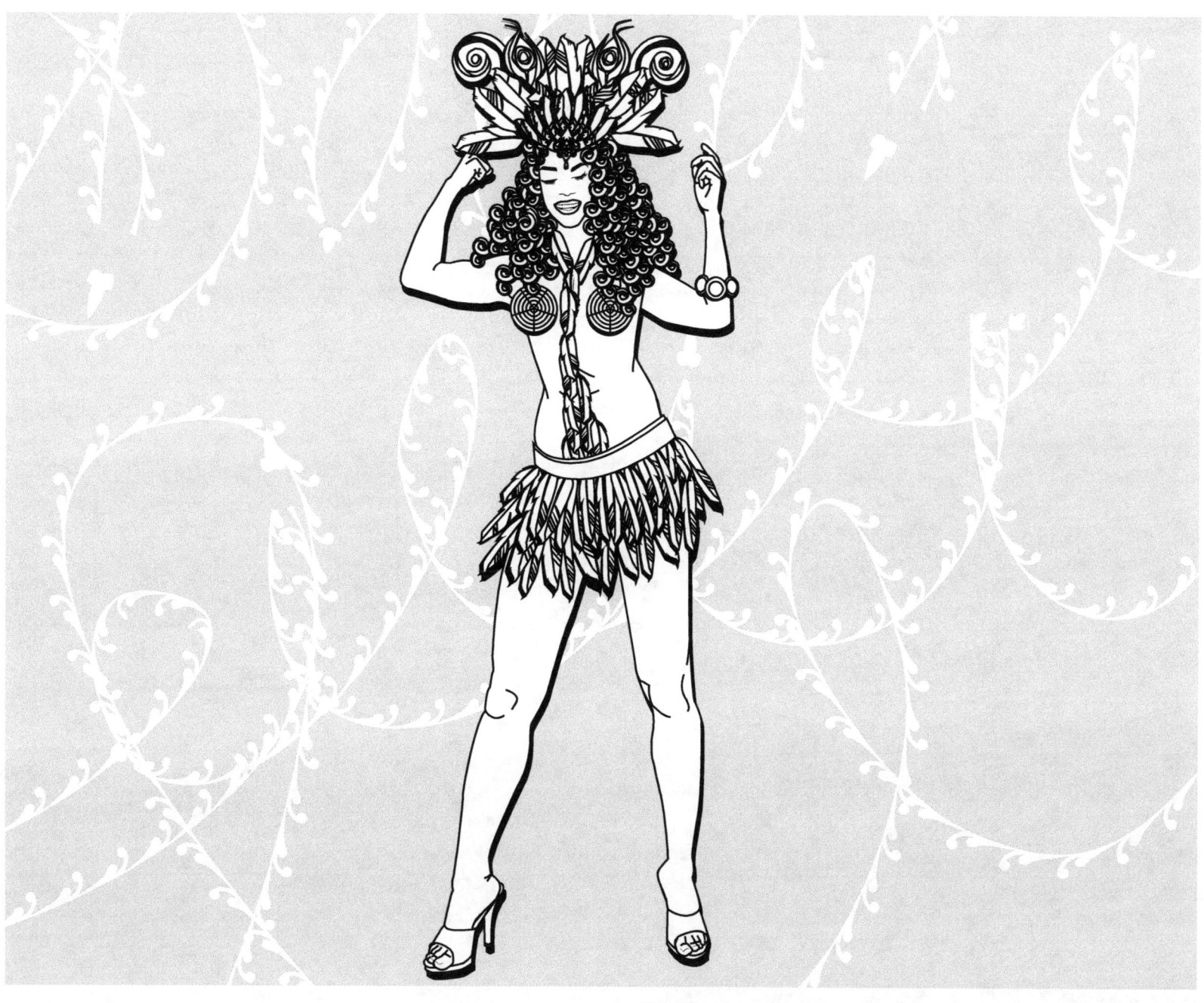

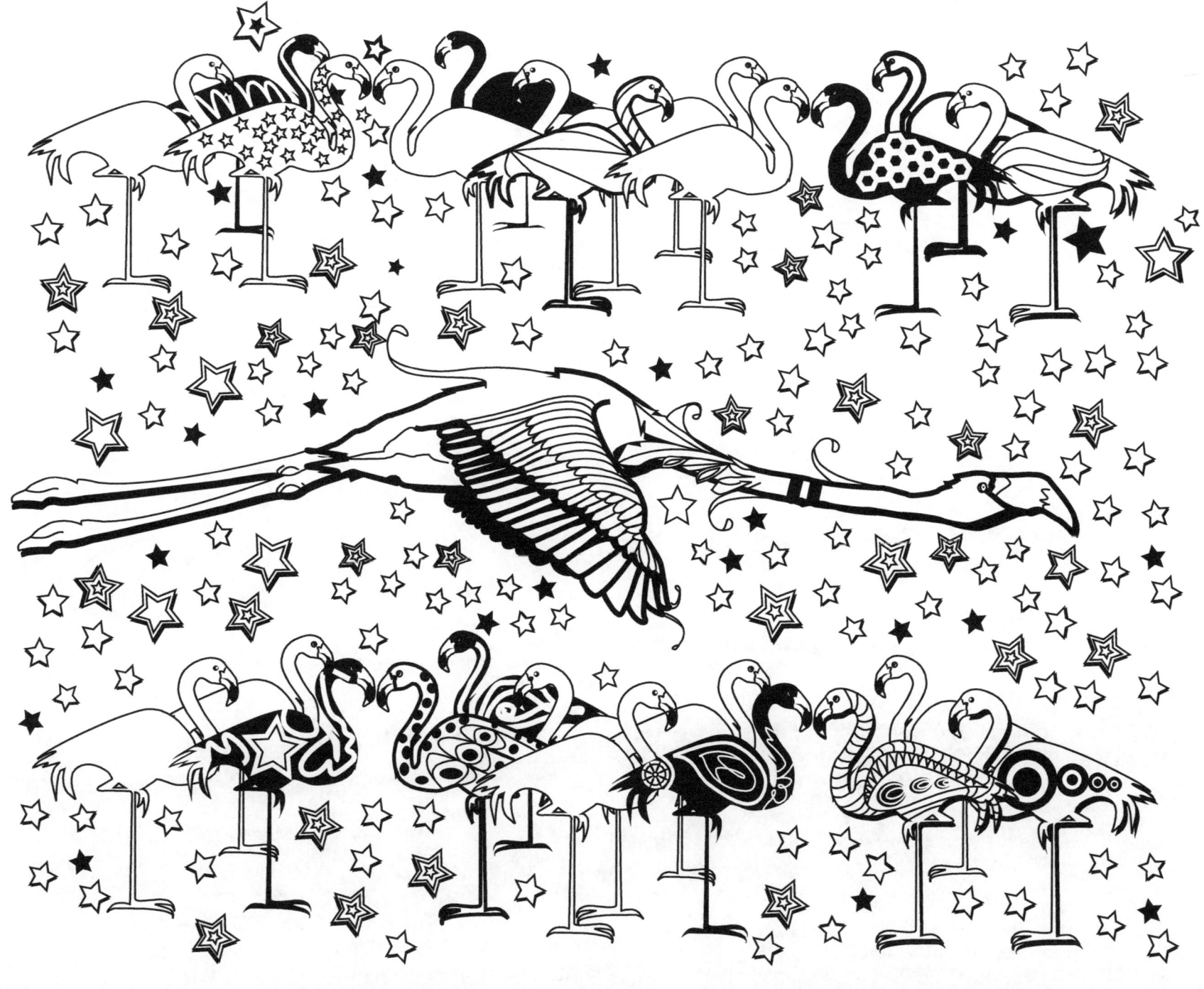

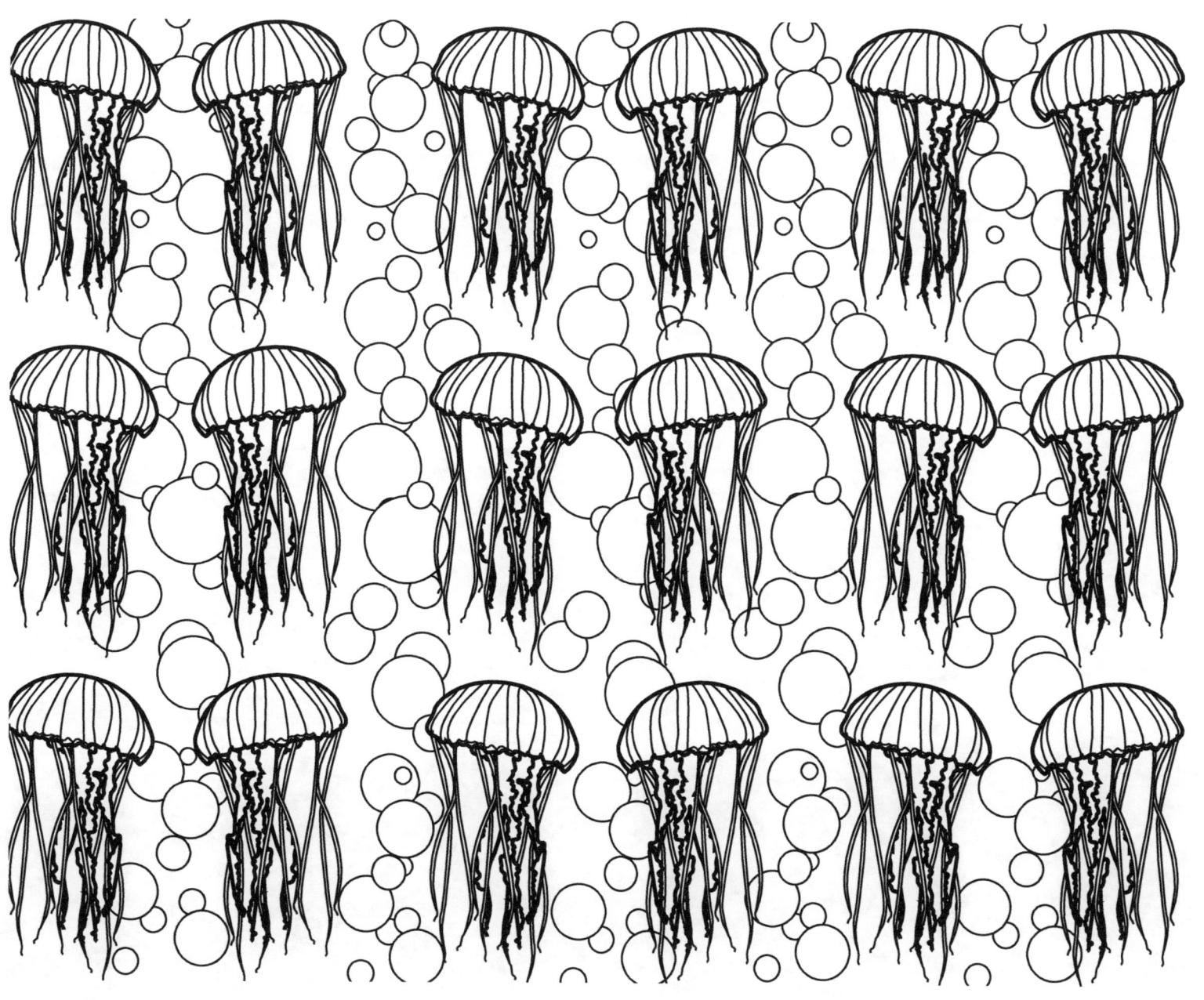

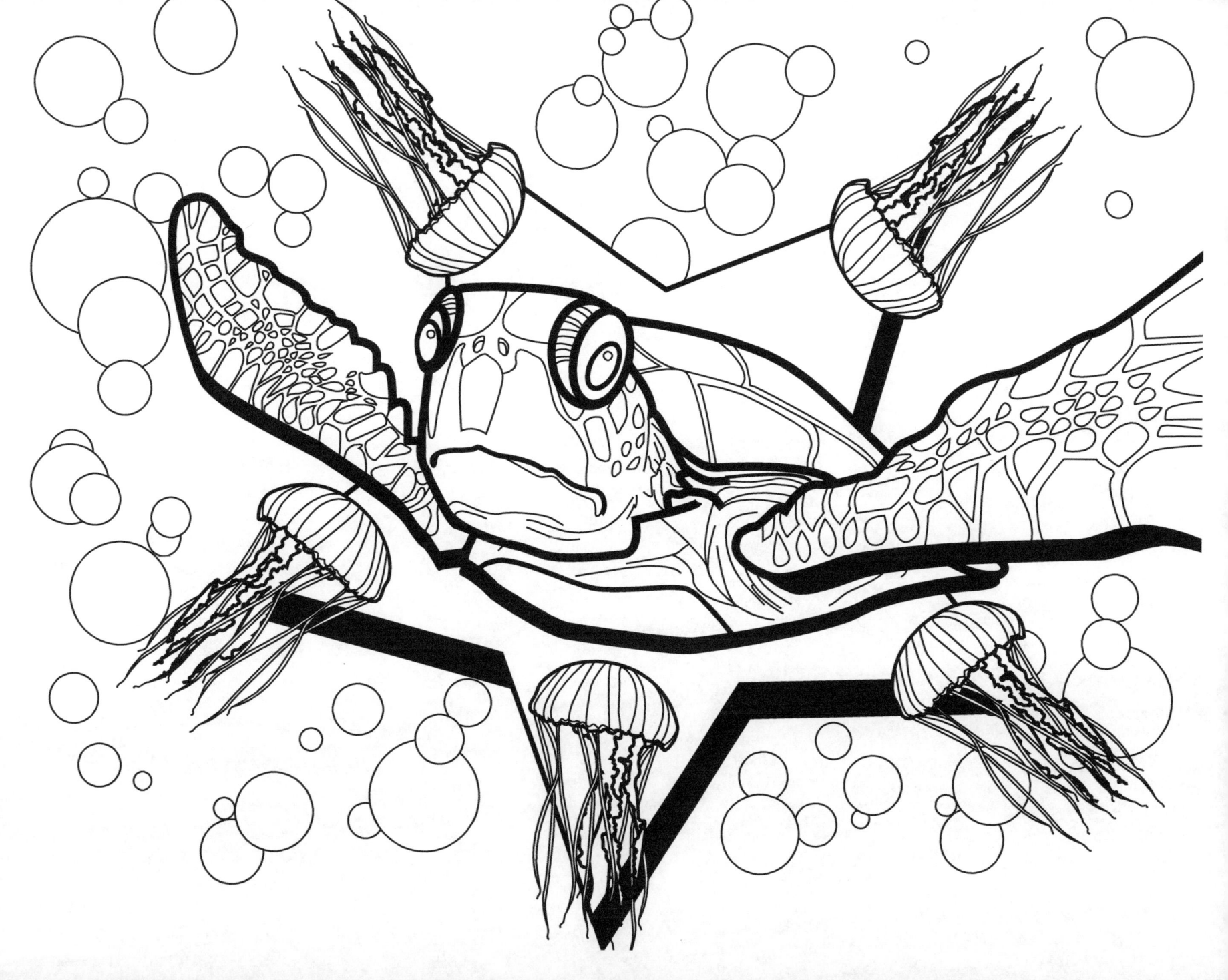

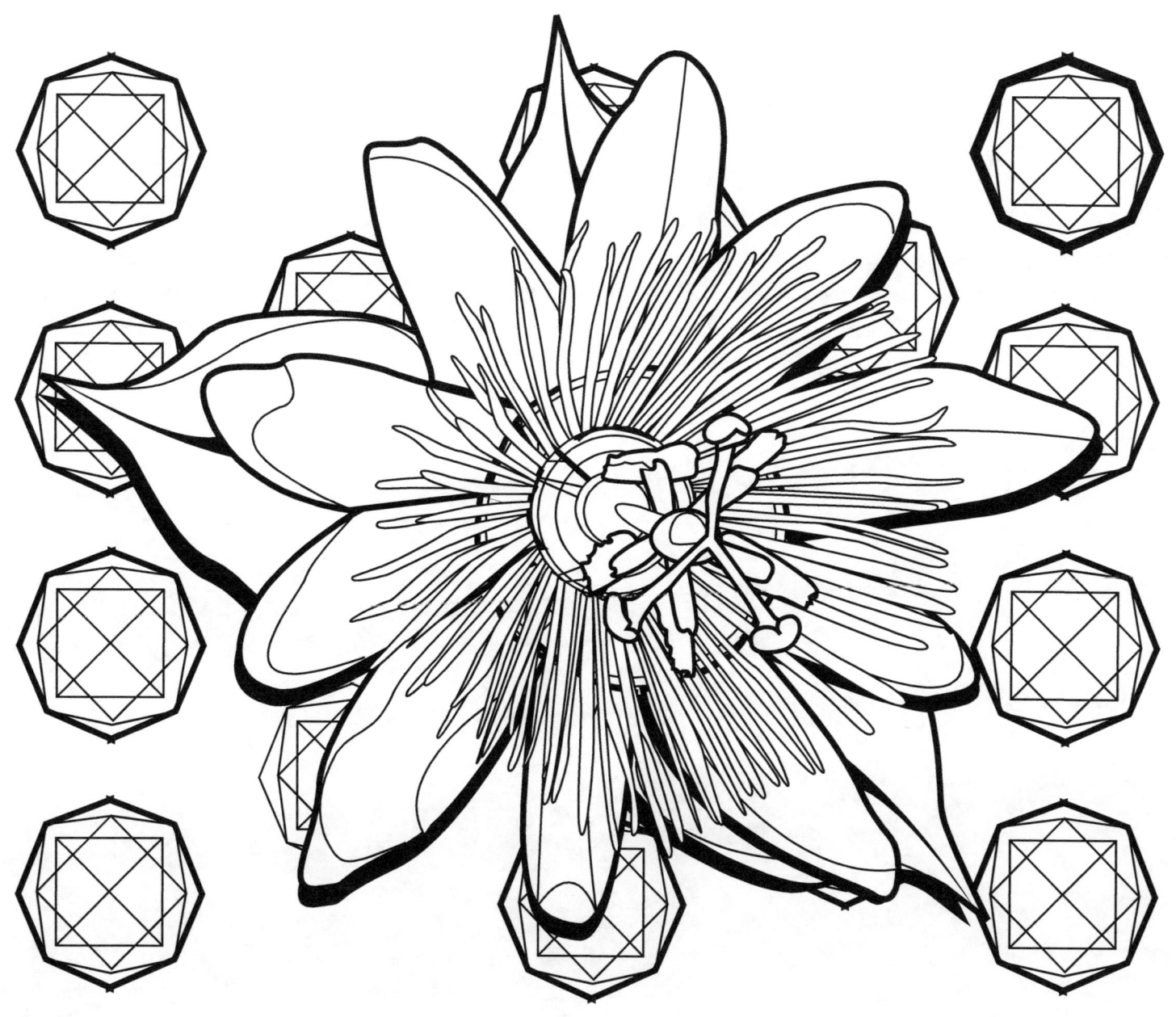

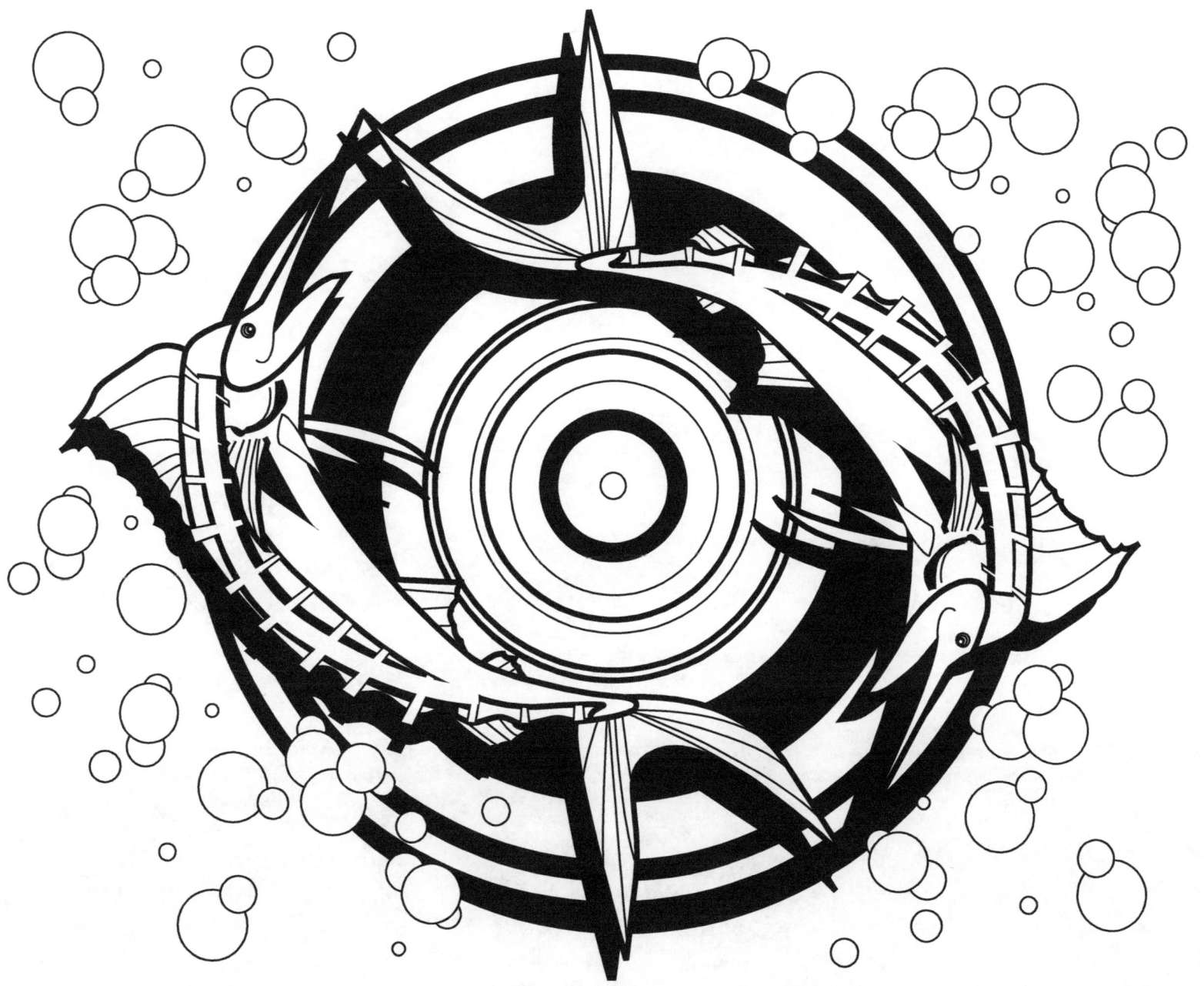

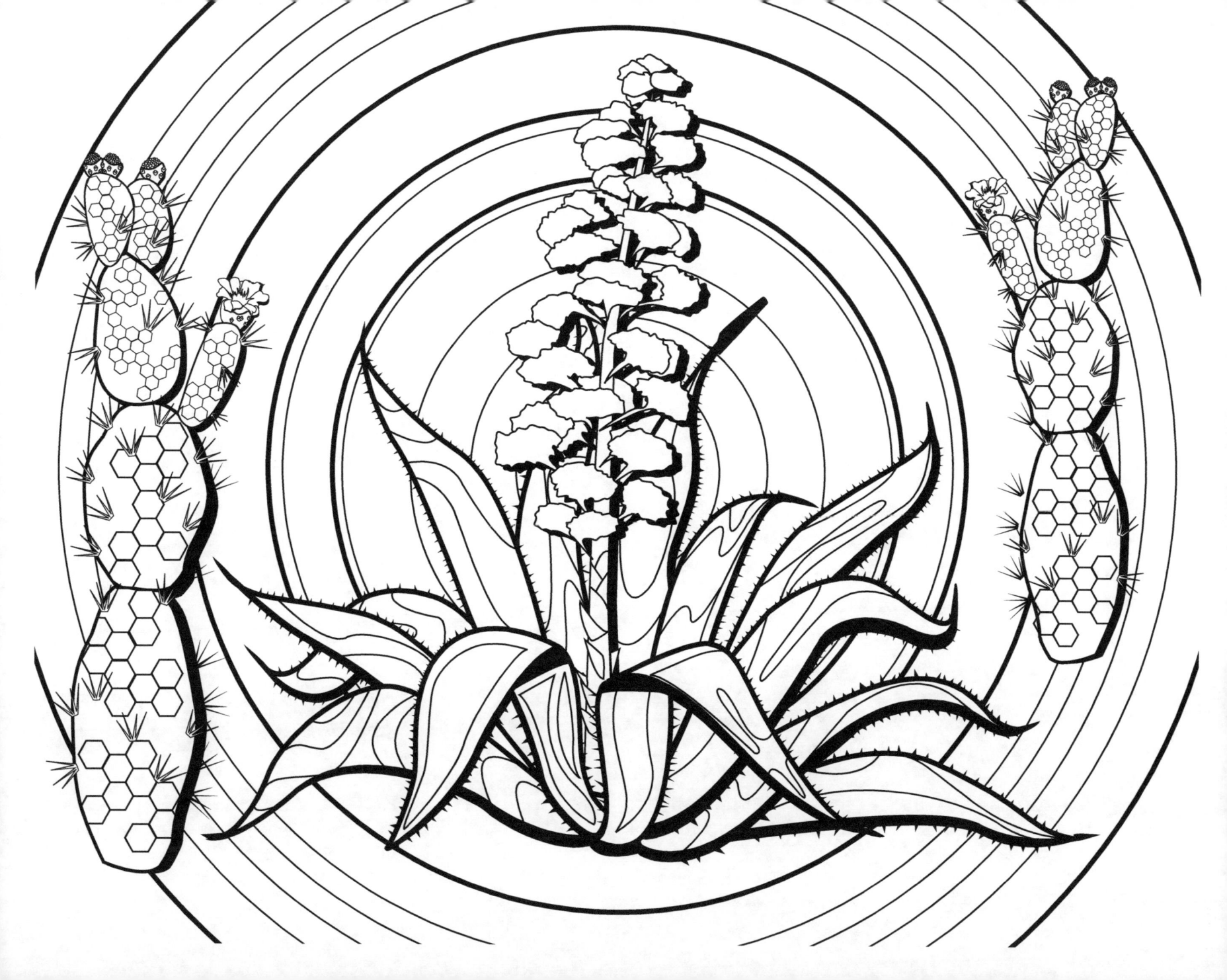

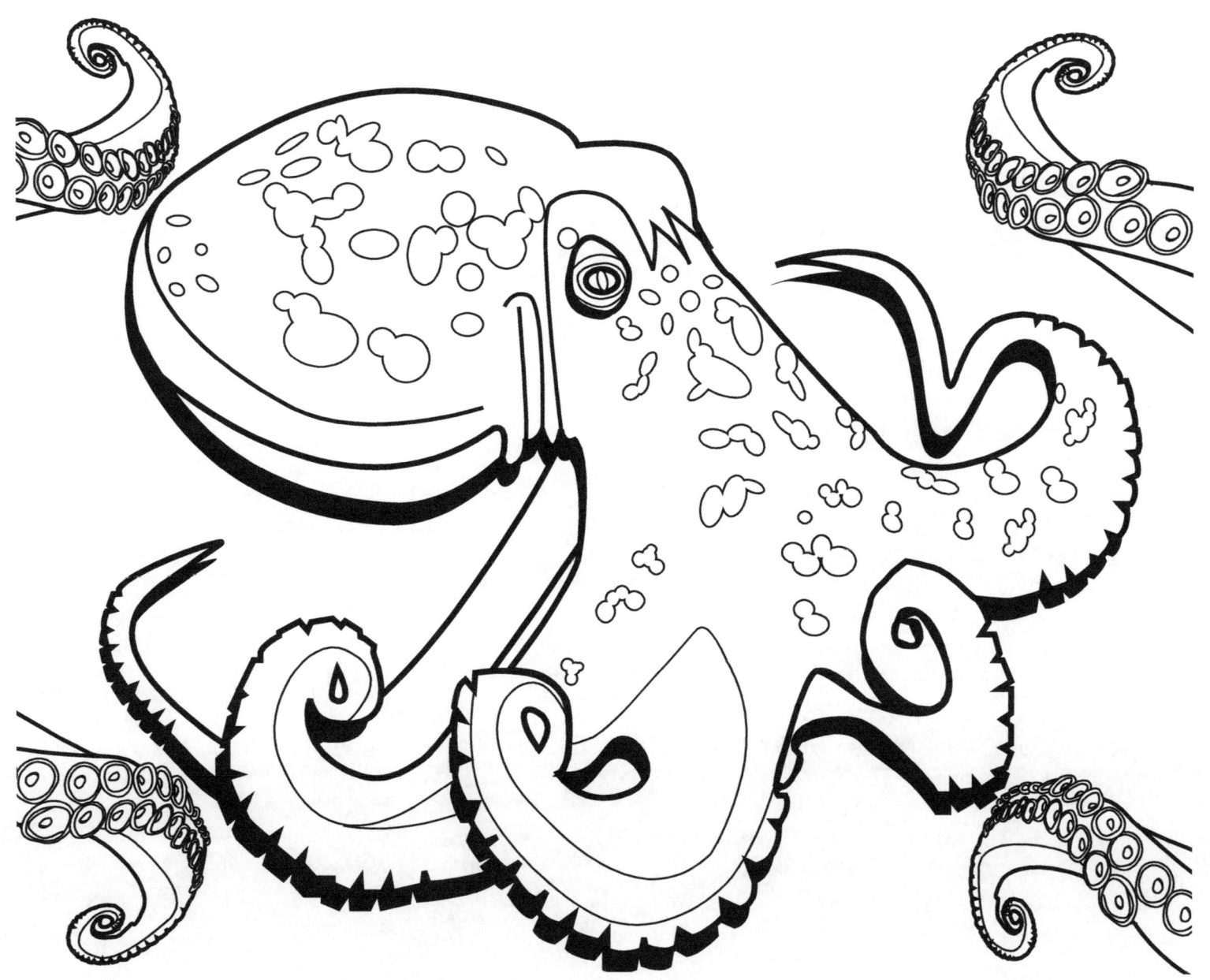

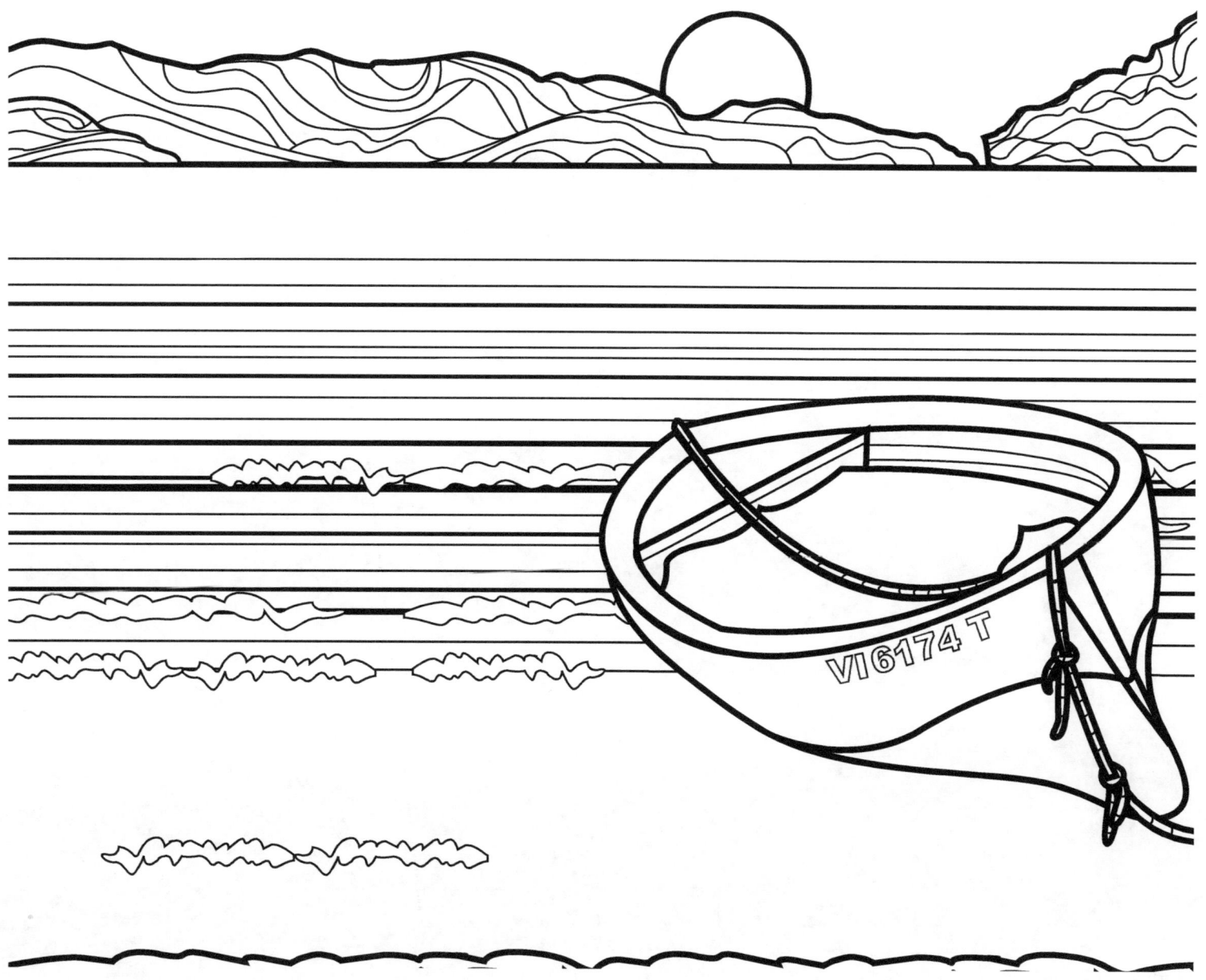

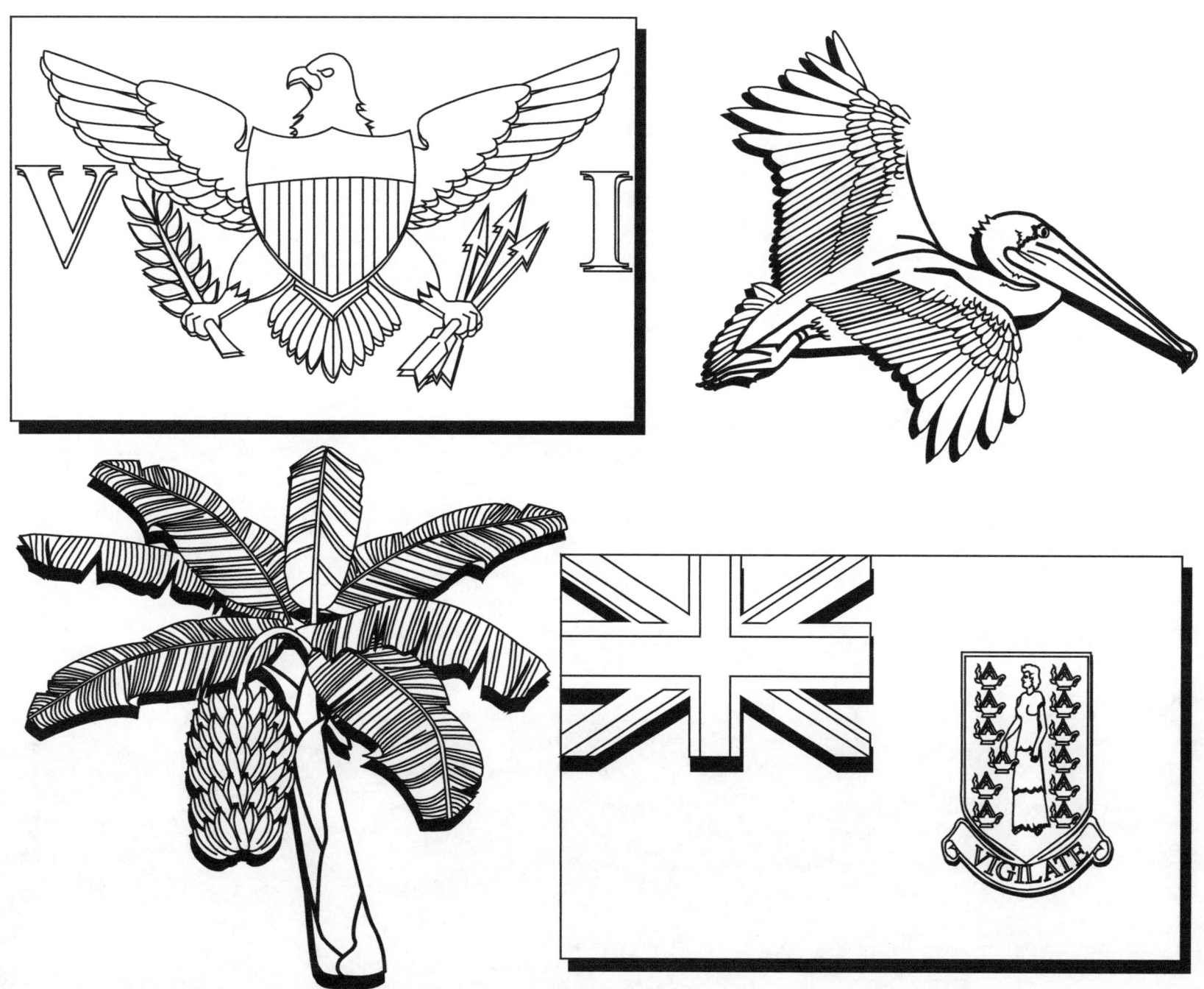

www.ingramcontent.com/pod-product-compliance
Lightning Source LLC
Chambersburg PA
CBHW080618180526
45168CB00007B/2963

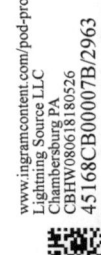